D1162185

This book is given in
love on the 20th occurrence
of your 55th birthday. ☺

Love,

Teresa
Rebecca
Ali
Logan

Clouds for the Table

Clouds for the Table

Collected Poems and Paintings of

SUSIE SIMS IRVIN

Providence House Publishers
WWW.PROVIDENCEHOUSE.COM
FRANKLIN, TENNESSEE

Copyright 2001 by Susie Sims Irvin

All rights reserved. Written permission must be secured from the publisher to use or reproduce any part of this book, except for brief quotations in critical reviews or articles.

Printed in China

11   10   09   08   07   2   3   4   5   6

Library of Congress Catalog Card Number: 2001091946

ISBN: 978-1-57736-242-5

Cover design by Elaine Kernea Wilson and Gary Bozeman
Cover painting by Susie Sims Irvin
Author photograph by Lauren Sims Campbell

PROVIDENCE HOUSE PUBLISHERS
238 Seaboard Lane • Franklin, Tennessee 37067
www.providencehouse.com
800-321-5692

To
Young people—everywhere.
God loves you.

Contents

Introduction

Clouds for the Table has many authors. They speak in tongues of tree and stone, of earth. The images walked these paths, roamed these hills long before our time. They were painted then in sunset and stream, in echo of gunshot and church bell. When I truly listen to them, *Clouds for the Table* is what I hear.

Why must I write, paint, publish? Because when I am still and open my heart, they—the words, the paint—are there. They cry for the light of day. The writings included in *Clouds for the Table* come from several collections of my work. *Shhh . . . It's Time for the Devotional* was published in 1981 and again in 1993, and *Falls Even Now the Seed* was published in 1993. This book also includes my new poetry of 1993–2001 and several poems and one painting from my life-changing journey to Israel and Egypt.

My poetry is intuitive. The image is its strength. At times these images gang up on me and lead to truths I had not suspected. It is my hope that you, the reader, will extend these thoughts to your own insightful conclusions— that the sound from these memories will reverberate through your memories and bring pleasure and discovery to your reading.

The paintings, oils from 1980–2001, veer wildly from abstraction to impressionism to expressionism as I search to find a style to record my journey. They have kept me alive, aware of what I am experiencing, and who I am. For the most part, they are rooted in the landscape and have been chosen for their synergistic relationship to the poetry—to illuminate, not illustrate, the written word—in the hope that you will discover that painting juxtaposed with poetry will create an added dimension of understanding.

I am most grateful to you who listened with me when my poems first appeared and learned to speak. You who gave me the courage to carry them farther. Family, neighbor, friend. Those precious ladies in the Daly Thompson Bible Class. Louise Morrison's writers, Stoneycrest Garden Club, the Study Club, Laura, Ann, and Jane. You are all part of what these words and paintings are trying so hard to be.

The Sewanee Writer's Conferences of 1994 and 1999 provided peak experiences for me. Just to breathe the same mountain air as our revered poet laureate, Robert Hass, and renowned poets Maxine Kumin, Andrew Hudgins, Rachel Hadas, Anthony Hecht, and Wyatt Prunty was heady stuff indeed. All write and teach from the highest rung on the ladder. To hear them read their magnificent words and then read my humble offerings was for me the pinnacle of literary success.

Equally nourishing have been the springs that fed my expression in paint—Gus Baker at the University of Tennessee, Nashville, certainly David LaDoux at Middle Tennessee State University, as well as the Vermont Studio School and now the Stonington, Maine Painters Workshop with John Imber.

There are other giants in my past and my present, but none stood taller than my father, Cecil Sims, at five feet four inches. I was only one of thousands who he taught to care deeply. To value the worth of each individual. To look beyond the superficial, probe beneath the surface for truth. He was seldom without a book in his hand, a twinkle in his eye.

Clouds for the Table would never have risen above the horizon without the expertise, enthusiasm, and compassion of Providence House Publishers. Andrew B. Miller and his incomparable team gave life to an idea and melded words and paint into a text that seemed preordained. I am forever grateful to them, especially Kelly Bainbridge, Elaine Kernea Wilson, Vanessa Hardy, and Pam Horne, for going far beyond professional excellence to create this joy that has made me infinitely proud.

It will be my honor and pleasure to enjoy your company in the lines you are about to read and the paintings you will encounter as you gather clouds for *your* table.

Clouds for the Table

Quiet Voices

Quiet voices clothe
Winter's jagged edge.
Doves murmur secrets
Under velvet breath.
Blurred hills stand still
Frozen to woolen sky.
Stand to wait in line *outside*
In freezing rain.

Black satin streams
Bathe themselves beneath
Down robes of snow.
Above their flowing nakedness
Whispers of vapor rise
To trace their sleek unwinding
Through muted browns
Of fields, laid by.

Night reads to himself
From poets of starlight.
Day gathers clouds
For the table.

Quiet voices need not speak
For those who listen
To hear, peace.

His Hands

Across the scrubbed maple
of our table,
I have watched
his hands grow old.

Seen the years back up
behind the joints,
turn smooth knuckle
to ridge of bone—
protrusions—
one by one.

I reach across now,
cover those years
with my hands.
To absorb the warmth
of slender fingers
that play my passions
as if delicately strung
upon some priceless harp.

I shudder with
the knowing
these forever *are*
his hands.
And I give them back.

Thrusting my own hands
into my lap.
Scolding them.
Too taken with the busyness
of doing they are.

I have seen his hands turn
red in the creases
raw with tending
our winters.

Close about a brown biscuit
on a white plate.
Push with ceremonial delight
new green peas
from our garden
onto his silver fork.

Tonight
his hands lie still.
Laid out large
upon the white sheet.
My hands slide
beneath his hands,
hoping to make them last
through the night.

I Feel So Much Closer

Love thy neighbors as thyself.

"I feel so much closer to you in winter,"
my neighbor said. "I can see your house from the road."
"And I can see out," I replied. "And up."
There are horizons we dared not believe in summer.
Distant hills we did not know. Paths that went unseen.

There is more space for God in winter.

Who is my neighbor, Lord?
His frost spreads evenly
across the night owl hooting
the den of scraggly fox
                    and across my home.
New snow records precisely
the blue-tinged trail of the black snake
the leap of rabbit from his burrow
                    and my footsteps.

Shadows lie flat across us all in winter.

Smoke from our neighbor's chimney
swirls with ours in winter sky,
falls in folds across
frozen pasture between.

We share the weight of winter, but the trees
carry its intensity up the hillsides on their backs.
Reach frostbitten fingertips to snare dollops of snow.
Dangle ice prisms from strings reflecting wet black.
Mauve. The purples winter alone can claim.

The cold is its own common denominator.

We feel the shiver from the shack
burned in the night. Of puffy birds
that dart. Icy post to icy post.
Of cows that wait. Silent heads down.
Eyes half-closed.

We are frozen in together. Neighbor to neighbor.

It is man who breaks ice
    on the watering trough
but it is wood from the oak
    that came down last summer
that warms his hearth,
    cooks his stew.

And surely it is God's design
that allows us to stand in wonder
at the clean curve of hill against sky
bare spine of wild rose bowed.
Stripped to simplest form.
Foundation upon which life must begin
if it is to bloom.

In winter
He takes us back to root.
Asks that we begin again.
Closer to Him.
In harmony with neighbor.

Above the slumbers of the town
Its crown of hills is rising—
Emeralds from nocturnal settings
Roused to float upon the mist
Of a morning just now
Making up its mind.

The hills mount then ride astride
The swells of dwindling pastureland
Begin their circling round and back again
An easy canter undulating across the horizon,
Propelling the white-headed town below, its
Unsuspecting hub curled comfortably in the lazy
Unwinding coils of the coffee brown Harpeth River.

Unaccustomed as it is to change
The town is waking now
To peer bleary-eyed into a thicket of growth
And it is growing more difficult each year
To keep Main Street corralled in the two blocks
That run from the Post Office
Down to where the Confederate Monument
Stands above it all—at ease,
Seemingly unperturbed as the latest invasion
Creeps over the hills through every pass.

The hills *do not know* what to make
Of that mall—its uncertain lineage—
Who pays her dues up front then sprawls
In unladylike fashion across the company counterpane
Mussing it with garish makeup
Casting her eyes a bit too often at the
Town wallet lying open upon the oak washstand.

The hills *do know* their time is coming but
Tend to look the other way—out toward
Nashville or Murfreesboro or Columbia
And their problems. They speak to each other
Only of the weather.

At Ease

The Tall Trees

naked they dance
against the dark hills
the tall trees
grope
big sisters grown too tall too soon
stretching slender arm
pointed finger
fastening hill
to sky
coupling
pulling earth up
a tufted counterpane
scalloped across the horizon
gathering life in its folds
little rivulets of town dribbling out
escape into the countryside

the roots of tall trees
go
deep
search
crumble granite
penetrate core
impelled
by the knowledge
that they are
the linchpins
that hold this
entirety
together

The Talent

the jagged red line
   digs painfully
      into flesh
   runs from heart
to head
   to heart again
          and out the fingertips
        does not perch there
waiting to be picked up
   whenever   a french bouquet
     to parade about the drawing room
      but glowers
          gut deep
          in darkest of pits
      lies coiled
   ready to strike
      and yet defiant. difficult
to coax to the surface.

it was what remained
   when the shell   a marriage
   broke   into   pieces
      left me shivering   blue
          nakedslackstooped
   three babes in arm
  only the jagged red line
          at our feet.
   O.K. O.K. O.K.
so I'll pick it   up
  return to square one
start on go
as in
    go back to school

            and I will stuff   whatever
I can get my hands on
into it
            and

            see what happens
        see if the worn seams burst
or if it floods
                    empty spaces.   takes over.

you have some skills.
            good. he said.
good. period.
                    but the next time after
        I did it over
    tearfully over persistently over
daringly over and over
                            his perfect eye
                    lit with surprise.
        good. he said. good work.
            the jagged red line
                    pulsed and glowed
florescent pink tentacle
                    flickering into depths unseen
and I knew.
            knew that I would feed it
        even as I myself
                        starved.

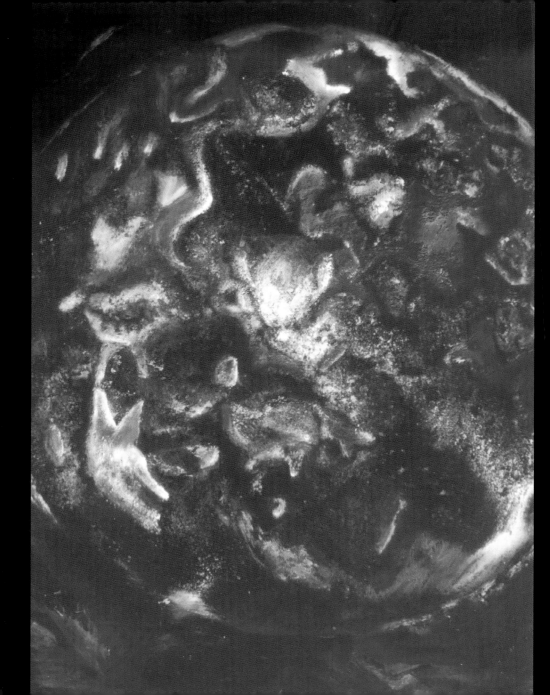

I hear the song of the morningbird
peal from my heart
note laid upon note
delicately diffused
into the thin clean air of winter.

I see my tears roll down your cheek
feel your smiles trespass across my face
and I begin to sense
that softest of lights
blurring boundaries
obliterating loneliness.

Boundaries

I mourn the cedar
that split and fell in the ice.
I am at pain
with the wounded the wasting old.
In agony
with the freezing flesh of the homeless.
But I begin to feel
these clean winter winds blow
through my barriers,
removing seals
I have so carefully placed on my life.

When the paths turned icy
I built a fence—locked the gate.
It is I who stepped off my perimeters
defined limits, denied access.

Now I wearily lay down
the piercing arrows of struggle.
Break across my knees
the anxious bow of striving
and holding out
these empty hands
begin to receive.

Stand Clear

Excuse me.
              Excuse me. Please.
I think this
              is where
I get off.

Yes, this is
              my floor.
As high
              as I go.

Stand clear as
              the door
closes
              behind me.

Petition

Did I come
to wear out?
To undo?
To break and scatter in bits and pieces
that which came to me whole?

Am I only the reaper
cutting the grain of my father's fields?
Devouring life?

My mind, my soul, my hands cry out.
They scream. They nag. They search
for one chunk of smooth hard clay
to scratch an arrow upon
one stone to chisel to let a stream run through.

To know that I was and was meant to be.

Turn me from years of growing fat
feeding upon others. An insatiable appetite.

Oh, Lord, I do not wish to return to this earth
with only bits of other desperate beings
between my capped teeth
beneath my painted nails.

The
New
Paintings

"These are very strange . . ."
he says it over . . . and over again
"very fine but very strange
like something you have brought back
from a place you have never been.
Perhaps the lining of your soul
is showing . . . turned inside out.
We don't know what they are."

a link a vision a free fall
a word unspoken
a sound unheard
at the edge looking in or
the real stretched out of focus

He does not know. I do not
know. Nobody knows
where they came from
where they are going.

I paint
and then I paint out
that which does not belong
and there they are
unveiled . . . have they always
been there?
Not mine.
Whose?

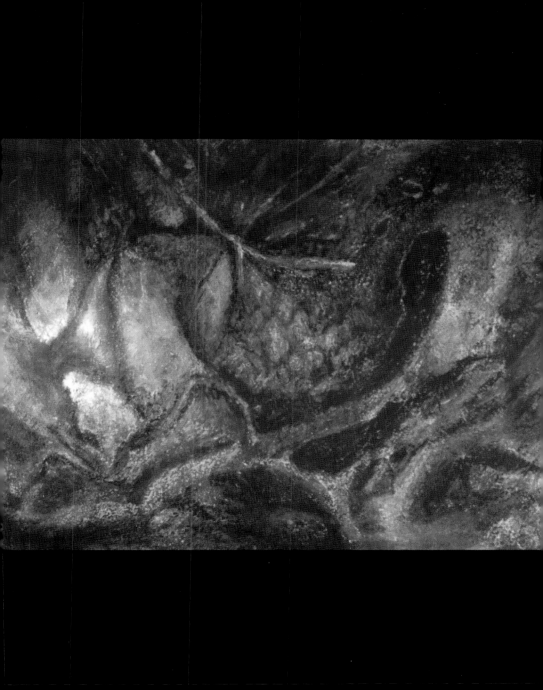

Reach

People slip through my grasp sometimes
back there where faded days
have started to brown around the edges.

This train is always moving.

We hold out our hands. Reach
but do not touch.

Both trains are going too fast.

Age

what utter use have you
for these tired but valiant cells
you steal from me
plucking them surreptitiously
painless suction in the dead of night
excavating silent empty spaces
gaping snaggled sanity
from struggling brain
where quickness and light
once put down roots
and confidently resided?

Age

be my guest,
inhabit some lesser organ
some robust limb
exact your quota
your daily vengeance there
leave be these carefully preserved
meticulously catalogued
remnants of mind
now so precariously perched
upon this dusty shelf
where they belong.

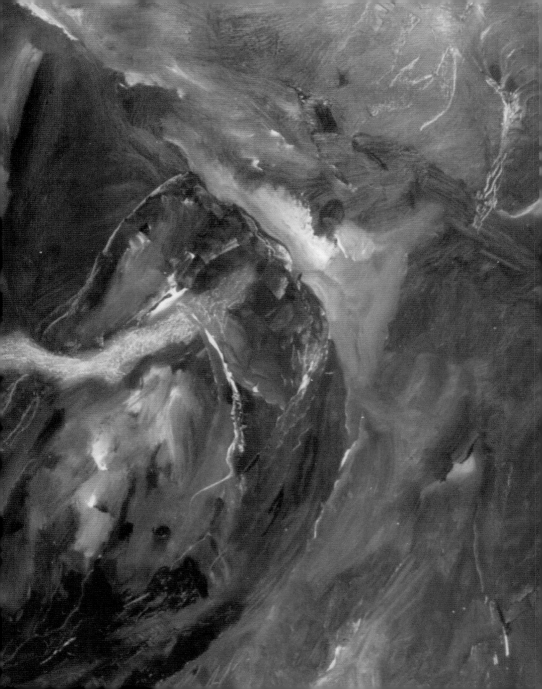

Friend

Friend

come help me find the thread
that unravels my soul
and sends cascading out
tangled knots
that choke and clog
and keep me bound
uptight.

Feelings

Up and down
their spiral staircase
they play beneath
this smooth exterior
that you and I call
Me.

Naked little gremlins
running their gamut
just out of reach,
playing havoc
with my controls.

Mischievously
punching tear buttons
when anyone can see
I am laughing.
Drawing back the curtain
to expose the aching heart
just when I had it all
covered up.

There now
you see they have fallen
and are hurt
after I had warned them
they were getting too close
to the edge.

I used to nurse them
protect and soothe them
keep a tight leash on each one
of my feelings.

But now that
I've gotten to know them
I'm rather intrigued
realizing
the sun is at the treetops
and they have so little time
left to play.

And so I only warily watch
as they run to hide
burying themselves in the sand
today,
dancing on my sleeve
tomorrow.
Now puffing me up
send me sailing
into a blue where
I have no business,
then puncturing hopes
dashing dreams.
Now fanning flames
then blowing cold breaths
on still-glowing embers.

Silly little feelings,
up and down
your spiral staircase
you play.
Each one a part of me.
And I,
all of *you*.

Prepare Him Room

Last week I awoke in the night
hearing words that were not my own
prepare Him room
prepare Him room.
Strangely satisfied that I now
had written a devotional
I went back to sleep
repeating the words
prepare Him room
So I would remember in the morning.

That morning our daily devotional read
"As we make our way through this Advent season,
we try to learn how best to welcome
this new King among us and
make Him glad He has come."

It all was beginning to fit together.
And then a wonderfully spirited British pastor
visiting in our pulpit ended his sermon—
"If you leave Jesus in the stable
you will miss much of this Christmas."
I knew then that the Lord
was writing this devotional
verse by verse.
That this year, Jesus
would be coming *here*
walking softly—sandalfoot
on these grey pine floors.
And every heart would be rearranging priorities
removing the clutter of small things
from the space marked
Reserved for our King.
Sweeping clean dark corners
shifting our lives about
to *prepare Him room.*

I understood then that Jesus
wanted most to be a part
of everything *we do now.*
He would be celebrating with us
going to our parties
sitting with us in our quiet
singing our carols
blessing our tables.

Jesus had come with us.
To this time and place.
We will welcome Him here now
and make Him glad He has come.
Joy to the world
the Lord has come.
Let every heart
prepare Him room
and heaven and nature sing
and heaven and nature sing.

To Christmas

Follow a star? Who me?
Follow a star? A map, maybe.
A good set of directions.
An arrow. But a star? In the sky?
On a dark night? Across a desert? No way.

And yet all of us here
Have been following this incredible star
For most of our lives. Across deserts.
Ravines. Over troubled waters. Treacherous paths
To mountain peaks. Pulled by faith
To the one real thing in our lives.

Each Christmas we feel that pull a little stronger.
Understand a little clearer this King of kings
Son of God reborn in us. This different King
Who came with answers to a world with only questions.
One who came to live among men. Teach them.
To show life as it could be. God as He was is.
And forever will be. To show us ourselves. Redeemed.
Radiant with expectations. Infinite possibilities.

No matter where we have wandered. What other kings
We have known. That star finds us. Leads us to a stable.
Each year we come a little earlier. More eagerly.
We stay a little longer. More fulfilled.
Soft hooves tamping a dirt floor.
Scent of hay. Baby's cry. Simple things.

Peace He gives to us. And warmth.
Love He brings to us. And joy.
We sing because we cannot help singing
We love because we cannot help loving.
We *have* followed a star. It has led us home.

Mary waits for us there
Waits now in the stable.
Does she call your name?

Do you hear her softly?
Down the crowded aisles
In the checkout lanes?
Threading holiday traffic
Following you home again?
Do you hear her softly?

Mary

Do you hear her clearly?
The voice of your littlest angel
When she begins to sing
In voices from childhood calling
Calling you by name
Do you hear her clearly?

Is that the light of Mary
Caught in your headlight beams
Igniting stained glass windows
Flickering upon your hearth?
Does she light the altar candles?
Spin the aura 'round your tree?

Do you leave your flock on the hillside?
Forsake your other kings?
Do you bring Him tears of gladness?
Weep love into the straw?
Do you sing your exultation?
Do you bring your name?

Mary waits for us there
Waits now in the stable.
Does she call your name?
Jesus is born for us there
Born now in a manger.
Does He know you came?

Front and Center

Quiet now—the house lights are dimming.
The conductor mounting the podium
awaiting the introduction
why—it is you!
You are the conductor of your Christmas.
You rap your baton to polite applause
your Christmas is well attended.
They've grown to expect a good performance.

Your arms sway
as you blend in reverence. Merriment.
The tree. Then praise. Soft candlelight.
Celebration. Quiet moments. Family
and friends. Good food. Prayer.
Memories. Other years. Other faces.
Tinsel. A few tears.
All in your own measure.
You set the tempo.
Build the crescendo.
Press the soft pedal.
It is an awesome task—orchestrating
your own Christmas.
There are moments of doubt
that all of this preparation might miss
become merely tinkling cymbals,
Sounding brass.

But there is Jesus front and center
a complimentary ticket.
It's His birthday, you know.
Shouldn't you dedicate this
performance to Him?
Or better yet—invite Him to the podium
and you take the front-row seat.
Aren't you a little tired of conducting?
Just think what He could do
for your Christmas.
He could really play it like it is.
No more doubt.
Angels you would hear on high.
And that little ember kept
buried in Christmas past would
become the flame that is Christmas present.

And the light shone all around Him
A standing ovation.
Those around you reach, shake your hand.
Yes, yes, thank you, that *was* Jesus.
Guest conductor of my best Christmas ever!

Poem to a Poet

I should know you now.
The rivers from your soul
have fed my bloodstream
all winter long.

And you have dug
deep fingers into
the pits of my past
dredging up all
my brothers with your brothers
my hollows with your hollows
my sundowns with your sundowns.

I should know you now
but the rivers from your soul
do not run backwards.

And the door to your passion
is but a mirror.

I am left alone with your child.
Conceived
by poetical insemination.

My Grandmother's Eyes

My grandmother's eyes burn charcoal holes
in my granddaughter's china face.
They are the same eyes I have worn
and her mother.
(My mother's eyes are blue.)
The stones of our eyes come attached
to roots that entwine
with unspeakable force about the depths
of heart and soul
or lie exposed and raw for others
to handle at will.

I hold this little granddaughter close
trying to tell her why
grey Chevrolet stationwagons
will become stagecoaches
teetering on the edges of canyons.
Why nights will be black stallions
she rides to white lather until
they rear, wheel, and snort
careening into backwater.

But my granddaughter's eyes reach through
the blurring browns of my own—through
the concerned eyes of her mother
going back to retrieve the spark
that ignited Granny's eyes
and dances there still . . . doing
a coquettish two-step
about the tip of my heart.

It is the season before the flower.
The lands wear a fringe of frosted sage.
Hillside cedars stand posted
muted sentinels.
Icy fingers starch
green lace collars.

*Waning of
Winter*

Naked. Crisscrossing.
Slender black branches hold back
the smothering white of down.
A February sky.

Two black crows slice through
plunk frozen tailfeathers
to gatepost. Caw. Tilt heads.
Listen for an echo.
Permission to leave.

Stone ledges jut. Ooze melts
from mossy pores. The purpled
Harpeth Hills hold winter in their palms.

Beneath man's frozen paths. Hiding places.
Already searching roots slither,
dart down deep crevices. Drawn
to buried waters running
clear through layers of past life.
Pregnant bulbs burst tender shoots
from swollen wombs. Heavy. Black.
The earth parts. Arches. Crumbles
against the thrust. New life.
It is the Silent Source emerging.
Into a wonder that will be spring.

This waning of winter
is for us also time for
dwelling with our Source.
Discovering undisclosed spirit
that will allow our lives
to flower. Thinned out. Pruned.
Transplanted. Divided from offshoots.
Tired of running rampant.

Each seeks to send up
a single delicate shoot. A
true statement of ourselves
the kingdom we serve.

Admonitions of Angels

See them crouch behind
the slave walls?
Hide down both sides
of Cotton Lane?
See them leave
single file?

Going to wait
on the hillsides.
Climb mountain slopes.
Reach with starvation's arm.
Grasp with finely webbed finger
tender tendril pushed into sky
pleading with any God
who will listen.

The trees knew
when the stragglers
were taken down from behind
when their thickets were invaded
to pluck the mightiest
from their midst.

But only the angels hear
the dying

and we seldom listen for
the admonitions of angels.

Untitled

I pray to the God
who hears above the roar
of the larger place
that pristine trickle
of each secluded spring
welling up from
untapped truth
imbedded
within each of us.

I pray to the God
who shifts
that last solitary stone
to release
our fertile freshness
forever to run unfettered.

Who stepping back
into the cool shade
of the damp bank
paternally watches
as the essence
of our uniqueness
emerges
in crystal clarity

and dares to enter
the wider stream.

Silently
this unlived moment
washes downstream
unnoticed,
lost, for all time.

Pale lives. Paler the dreams
imprisoned in polished white skulls
anemic shadows shrinking to fit.

Unlined

Passion sizzles briefly.
Look again.
It has fizzled away.
The pot is dry.

While silently,
another unlived moment
washes downstream
and is lost
for all time.

Thought cools on the back burner
to politically correct temperatures
floats aimlessly . . . dallies on the surface
refusing to be pinned down

Resistant to all stains
failures . . . dares . . . possibilities
genetically engineered of sterile components
to project no conflict . . . go either way
make no waves.

While silently
another unlived moment
has washed downstream
unnoticed
lost, for all time.

PRAYER FOR PEACE
BY SAINT FRANCIS ASSISI

Lord, make me an instrument of your peace,
Where there is hatred, let me sow love;
where there is injury, pardon;
where there is doubt, faith;
where there is despair, hope;
where there is darkness, light;
where there is sadness, joy;

O Divine Master, grant that I
may not so much seek to
be consoled as to console;
to be understood as to understand;
to be loved as to love.

For it is in giving that we receive;
it is in pardoning that we are pardoned;
and it is in dying that we are born to eternal life.

Amen

SALESIAN MISSIONS
2 LEFEVRE LANE • NEW ROCHELLE, NY 10801

From my chair
across the breakfast table
my looking out
evenly divides
into windowpanes.

One view
sliced up and down
and across
empty squares
tic tac toe.
Neatly framed fragments
    climbing limbs dipped in sky
    three stepping stones slightly tilted
    the bumped corner on our porch swing
constants in my life.

Black coffee sloshes cold
against my shiny white mug.
The phone rings.
Rings again.
Day begins.

Windowpanes become
    turning kaleidoscopes
    tossing familiar patterns
    into tinted racing blurs
changes in my life.

Caution:
windowpanes are good only
as temporary dividers
to looking out
as long as one stays seated
throughout the entire performance.

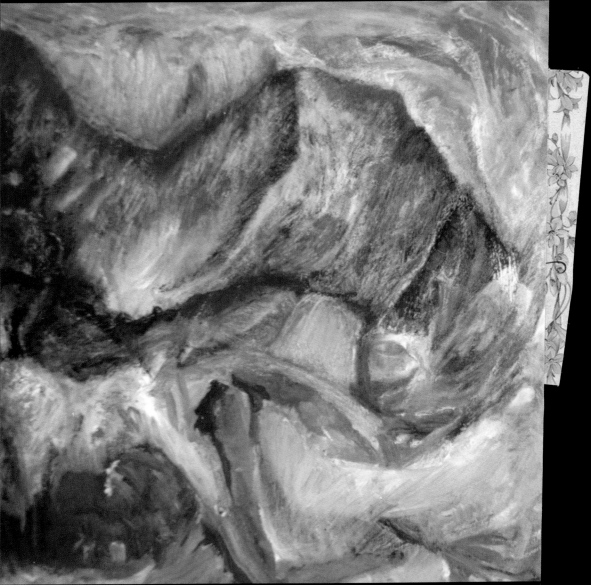

In His Shadow

I did not even know they were there
when I went to pick the buttercups.

We had missed the pileated woodpeckers
and noticed the owls
on farther down the hill.

Until my three baskets trembled
with the intensity of fluted gold
I did not know why.

Nearing the crest of the hill
where the last King Oak lay fallen
bulbs happily nestled in crumbled life.

I heard and knew the swooshing
felt his menacing shadow encompass me
drawing breath chilling blood to bone.

Instinctive hands shielded my face
I crouched to escape tensing of talons
cowered prey beneath hovering predator.

In stealthy silence he circled just above me
naked head down beady eyes riveted.

Then another lumbering awkwardly
from her confinement to a perch
above young or eggs perhaps.

Abandoning my treasure
engaging the other with my gaze
I backed from beneath his shadow.

Quickly threaded trembling steps
down between the mossy ledges
made treacherous by spring rains.

I would come back for the buttercups.
Bring someone with me
someone with a wary eye. Someone
who would like to pick buttercups
growing a golden ring around a hill
where my mother had planted them fifty years ago.

Planted in the vain hope
that my brother would come home from war
to build his dream within her ribbon of gold.

Instead we hung a gold star in our window
turned the lights down low
and pulled the shades.

I would come back and bring someone
someone who understands about brothers
someone who has never seen vultures up close
someone with a broom.

Trespass,
Trespass

In the stillness of now
In the russet/brown color of marsh
Red-winged blackbird is nested.

In spotless white Nikes
yellow billcap, spyglass
intruder encroaches.

Close. Closer. Close. Closer.

Trespass.   Trespass.
Blackbird Territory
blackbird territory.

Spyglass focused, so perfectly focused
Red-winged blackbird flushed
From three tiny eggs, speckled blue.

Feathers flutter rage. Black/red rage
Wings knock on grey sky.
Sky opens. Swallows blackbird.

Three tiny secrets, family secrets. Grow cold.
Spotless white Nikes retreat. Muddy.
All muddy—the russet/brown color of marsh.

Ode to a Hill

I lived then on the slope of my hill.
The dirt road went to the top
of the rise and stopped
where the hill leaned forward
shadowing
the fertile tenderness of the fields.

At sunrise she draped morning mist
about her shoulders
and took her seat in the family circle of hills
that rimmed my days and collected my years.

Clasping me willingly
to breasts of strength and constancy
drawing my dreams up to her
up past the treeline
she reached to launch my thoughts
from branching fingertips
laughing with me as they floated freely on sky
then dove wildly
crazy windless kites careening into cloud.

I lay upon her then
cradled in thick moss
that grew beneath the tall cedars
looked up through green lace
into clearest blue
and whispered *Mother*.

Behold

Early each spring
Out in the garden
My fiesty little Granny
Sings "In the Gloaming"
When the pink notes
Pop open up and down
The willowy branches of
Her flowering almond bush.

Early each spring
Out in the garden
My fiesty little Granny
Sashays across my heart—
Sinking spiked heels (size four)
Deep into the fertile warming
Of my soul.

They called last night
over icy black lines—stretched—taut
reaching across the mountains
from North Carolina to Tennessee
voices high-pitched . . . urgent.

Their first.
She arranging her final weeks
heavy . . . expectant . . . anticipating.
He staying out of the way
cleaning . . . rehearsing . . . feathering.

Blood Lines

"We need the names
the old family names
embroidered names from those
samplers . . . pillowcases . . . quilts
in the Steele Bible
from the Radcliffe stones."

The line pulses red now
doubling back across the mountains
from whence it came
drawn by oxen
five generations ago.

"Shearer . . . Dabney . . . Rebecca . . ."
our line extending
"Alexander . . . Matthew . . . Grace . . ."
inching one baby-step further
back across those mountains.

"Ratcliffe . . . Scales . . . Mozelle . . .
Did I say . . . Inez?"
Stitching new to old
updating . . . projecting
"Nancy . . . Sims . . . Wilson . . ."

A new branch buds beneath the bark
and waits there throbbing.

Morning sprawls
across the earth's belly.
Flung with breath sucked in
into that suspended moment
when nothing new is
and everything new becomes.

The cord is cut and life cries from the cradle.
Darkness relinquishes contours,
form rooting into form.
The lingering etch of the cricket call soars,
then sinks within the brain.
Twittering pillow talk from nesting birds
bubbles out between layers of quiet.

Dayborn

Tenderest branches sway,
then sweep into crescendo,
rippling down fence rows.
Dry leaves—skewered
rattle breath into new day
awaken feeling beneath my challis robe.

Mist gathers in folds.
Seams of sunlight glide in on rollers
to lean against tree trunks,
usurping seats vacated by shadow.
The rotted limb ricochets . . . thuds
simultaneously stabs earth . . . quiet.

Caw-Caw mocks the common crow.

The seal is broken.
The babe cannot forever stay at breast.

Into the gaping furrow
laid open by the blade
falls even now the seed.

Prose/Poem

Heart-flung ecstasies pealed upon the springday . . . calling me to the rail fence. . . . So unaffected they were . . . they might have echoed from her crib. Instead she stood widelegged ankledeep . . . set down in the vast front clover field.

The tissue blue of the kite . . . dove in wild arcs swished its gingham tail at the bluer sky . . . china hands instinctively played upon its spool, a musician . . . head tilted . . . reading a score inscribed upon the heart.

I stepped beneath the cool dark cedars . . . sensing my intrusion upon a private joy . . . when a sudden gust carried the thin brown legs swiftly past me. The delicate pink of her blouse ballooned behind . . . beneath strands of brown hair trailing life . . . sun . . . youth . . . spring. . . . I gasped with helplessness a mother's fleeting image . . . fearful . . . lest she too be borne aloft . . . beyond a world that had so easily bruised her fragile soul.

The inevitable fence confined her flight. She leaned into barbed wire . . . pulled toward new largeness she felt . . . clasped briefly the cord ends to her . . . threw both arms aloft . . . released her hold . . . stood frozen there.

"Good," I said aloud to myself . . . to the cedars. "I would never have let go. I would have struggled against the wind . . . brought it back in . . . tattered . . . saved it . . . patched it up . . . trying to wring one more joy from a tired old kite." Perhaps the same chord was not imbedded . . . binding her to the familiar . . . vulnerable to the pain of letting go.

"Good," I said again, stepping from the cedars . . . waving my floppy hat as she turned and headed back to the house. Seeing me she pointed over her shoulder at the receding kite . . . thrust both hands over her head in triumph. She called, "I let it go!"

Those White Lilies

Oh! for goodness sake
will you please come here
those white lilies are making
a real spectacle of themselves
blooming all over each other
climbing right out of their crystal vase.

See them twitter behind those pushy petals
burnt orange stamen trembling to the touch
such transparent ladies-in-waiting
how they jostle for approval
before that gilded mirror.

But who will remember
even one of these pretty faces
tomorrow—
when the new buds
begin their bloom?

Letter from Springtime

Dear One,
Oh! you will never ever guess . . . this time.
Today I found a hole in the sky
with my name on it.

So, crossing my arms
over my chest
and pointing my toes,
I twitched my nose (the way you say I do)
and rose straight away up its shaft
sitting on a soft breeze
riding on a song.
I stopped at the first waterfall
and watched a sunbeam
fold my body seven times
and slip it into the drawer
of a passing cloud.

Here thought wears my face,
a caress has my fingertips,
a heartbeat measures all ingredients.
Correct decisions
are scattered like rose petals.
Instructions gathered daily
and pushed over the side.
Judgment runs off quickly
and worry drops straight through.
A new roll of time is automatically
inserted upon request.
Signs point to nowhere in particular.
I shall probably stay
even longer than
forsythia sprays yellow and
streams bubble blue.

To find me:
Turn left into springtime
four somersaults from the first tulip
and look up.

This Is the Morning

This is the morning.
You know it even before you get out of bed.
That April morning when sun outlines
the pattern of your bedspread then
sends elongated tracings of windowpane
to climb the opposite wall.

It is a little too wet. A little too cold
a little too early but your heart
is ready to burst with buds
of red tulip. Grape hyacinth.

You find yourself speaking to the dog.
Conversing with the cat. Even nodding
to a passing bee as you sort
through handles worn to smooth
for your favorite rake.

Not one moment longer are you able
to resist the delicate blue of vinca blossoms,
playing hide-and-seek through new green leaves,
the decisive Stars of David. Little choir
of white singing from a mossy rock.

This winter has not been as bad as some
but brown leaves from the big oak
   lie deep against old brick borders.
And lichen, grey bark, twig
   have accumulated between frosted blades
of young iris. The debris of winter—
at once protecting, inhibiting new growth.

Metal prongs dig deep
into rich brown mulch. Reach moist
charcoaled earth beneath. Lay it bare.
Open to first light. Warmth.
You can almost feel it heave.

And then there they are.
Tenderly inscribed. Emerald green. White transparencies.
Unwind before your very eyes. Spring's new shoots.

You feel a great affection.
Too large for the human heart.
What God must feel when we come through
winters of our lives after lying dormant
under great piles of self-pity. Isolation. Brooding.
Debris of our winters. Protective covering
we heap on ourselves. Shielding yet stifling
the light, the love of God.

How He must rejoice seeing us stretch
as He turns back that under which we lie buried
to find us vulnerable. Yet open.
It is done. The bed as neatly groomed as
a four-year-old son emerging from the barbershop.

We stoop to load that last bit of twigs
into that last black plastic bag.
Realize how much of the leavings of winter
have slipped through the rake.
Lie crumbled now about new plants.
Storms of winter reduced to nature's mulch.

So it must be with our winters.
Each leaves behind its potion
    enriching our lives
    for seasons to come.
Hallelujah and welcome
    twisted little red peony
    fuzzy little primrose
    spindly little phlox.
God lives
    and will sing a new song
    through us all.

Spring is here. Praise the Lord!

Dark slender natives diving headlong into undergrowth

Paths take off unannounced
where other feet have led
when left to their own devices.
Slide deep into untrampled greens
branch from sterile plotted pavement
of public places.

Paths

I remember the shortcut
that stretched across our mountaintop.
Twin bands of red clay
padded with pine
randomly studded with mica chips.
Flickering sunlight and shadow
dappled its silence.

Yellow lilies sprang from banks.
Rhododendron and mountain laurel
bloomed twice taller than we.
Wild blueberries ripened
beneath the idle rust
of a forgotten water tower.
A secret carved-out place
too shy for the glare of openness.

A cloistered ambling place
just long enough for loitering undisclosed
secluded intimacy careless laughter
the caressing of private untampered-with moments
where thought became idea
idea acquired face
crystallized
and imprinted forever
our other paths.

Here

If it is just the same
With you
I will leave
You, here.

Right here
In this place
Where the trees
Embrace to shield
The yielding path.
And stone spreads
Cool fingers out
From skirt
Of underbrush.

You go on.
Follow the voices
Of others up ahead.
I'll just stop
To catch my breath
Here—where I am.

A Bad Day in the Hospital

Your flowers bloom too loudly
strain too hard against the bars
of that ceramic cell.
They scream at me,
an outlandish bouquet swished
from beneath
the magician's velvet cape.

You bring them at their peak.
There are no buds.
Must I discern
their daily dying,
preside over their demise?
I hereby decline. Let them be.

They must surely prefer
to shed all that garishness
in private . . . quietly . . . discreetly
to drop a muted wreath
about their feet
dry petals upon polished wood.

Do not bring the dustpan
for their potpourri.
We may yet stir some kinship
strike some milieu . . . a harmony
dwelling here together
among our leavings.

Tomorrow bring me seed.
A bucket of loose loam
to crumble in our hands
feed upon the sprouting
in our souls and perhaps
with patience
in God's time
we'll have
a bloom.

It is May.
Each morning
holds out a fresh bouquet.

May is bloom. Profusion of bloom.
Peach iris. Blue phlox. Creamy peony.
Deep red rose. Pink sedum. Lavender foxglove.
And daisies, daisies everywhere.
Chasing butterflies down back lanes.
Across fields carpeted in white clover
fringed blue with ragged robins.
Pink briar roses cascade from fence posts
and white ones spew still fountains
through the deep cool of green woods.

May is greening. Densing of green. Fullness.
Leaf on leaf. Light green on dark green.
Green to softened edges. Sculptures in green.
Shading. Enlarging hillsides. Hearts.

May is growth. Black soil wears a ruffled collar.
Yellow-green lettuce leaves about
even rows of spring onions. Tractors plow. Plant.
New hay ripples. Overflows white fences.

May is life. Life in abundance.
Chestnut filly. Her blaze sunlit.
Four white stockings race the wind.
Three black kittens open blue eyes.
Hiss at the world.

I came that you might have life
and have it more abundantly.
Life in profusion. Productive life.
Life in bloom. Life in May.
       Lord, let us live it.
       Let us live it together.

It Is
May

*Reunion
Hillsboro
High
Class of
1945*

Yesterday danced
in eyes grown more kind
with caring.

Lives turned lovely. Turning still.
Creep into bounds of maturity.
Feel at home there.

Time erasing time.

Full hearts revealed.
Wrapped in tissue paper.
To be opened gently.

Laughter
delightfully
never drained
of its silliness.

Memory
sifted through years
indelibly, incredibly
keeps us forever
part of this whole.

Life pressed into life
pieces fitting together.
We know it.
We *all* know it.
And we laugh once more
together . . . at ourselves.

Because at last
we can *be*
just ourselves
together.

—For those who no longer answer roll call,
"We hold your place . . . in line."

"Mama. Mama
Turn off the dark."
Pry loose the clenched fists
Screwed into the powder blue bars
Of my childhood.

Mama,
Mama

"I'm here. I'm here."
The rose pink lamp
On your night table
Clicks on in your sleep.
A sliver of light slides beneath
The door closed between us.

"I'm here. I'm here, Mama."
But the rose pink lamp
Still on your night table
Will not shine through your darkness
Nor take away the bars of
Your bed raised between us.

Will not stem the flow
That empties your mind,
Running, running over,
Too much for my cupped hands.
It leaks
Through the crack
In my heart.

"Mom. Mom."
When the rose pink lamp
Clicks on in *my* home now
It's *your* love, Mama,
that stills my grandchild's fear.
"Mom. Mom."
"I'm here. I'm here."

As a child
I always knew right where God was
at least at night
I did.

When dark came in
the windows of
the pink sleeping porch
next to Mama's room
the white net curtains blew
out from the wall
shades slapped their window frames
and I took hold
of two spindles on the headboard
of my little iron bed painted blue
squeezed them tight
closed my eyes
and waited for the train.

I could hear the whistle
as it started out Harding Road
past Mr. Hill's waterfall
past Richland Creek
past Nine Mile Hill
out past anywhere
I'd ever been before
carrying me
up
up and around
up and around
and around
like up the round green steps to
the Ladies Dressing Room
at the Belle Meade Country Club
only more up

God's
Place

up past rooftops
up over big trees
up through stars
until finally I could see
behind the moon
and there He would be
sitting there
everynight
just like the King of England
sitting in my father's blue velvet chair
sitting there waiting for *me*.

I never saw any angels or people up there.
Never ever had to wait in line.
I never even thought about Him
having to be God to anybody else.
I just came to tell Him
everynight
all those things
I thought about.

I never did remember
the
coming
down
I just supposed
God put me back
everynight
because
I always always
was there
in the morning.

The River

I live in the bend of the river.
She circles round behind me
and holds me in.

My front fields lead out to the highway
but coming home is to the river.

She is my good neighbor
who just keeps riding by
sometimes laughing as she slings
whitewater down rapids
or lazily rolls over drifting logs
sometimes sliding by smoothlike
a lady whose white birches arch
over her . . . wild buttercup and phlox
press in upon her thighs.

It is summer now.
She lies flat
rocky ribs gape as she retches
over stagnant pool, warm green scum
and buzzing dragonfly.

But winter rains resuscitate and
soon she will sneak past the rock wall
sprawl across the low fields.
Shimmer like a sunning snake.
Claim *these too are yet mine.*

Resigned

Old animals
(a pair)
circle
stiff-legged
tails clinging
coats matted . . . missing . . .
nudging each other on.

Circle again
to root out all possibilities
sigh, then sink heavily
into the certainty of down
and nose in
rolling somber eyes up
to ask just once more
for the period that
goes at the end.

Get Back!

Out from under the cedars
Embroidered across the ridge
Of the Warner Park hills
The junior-high cross-country
Girls are coming.
Preteens broadcast in primary colors,
Confetti littering the quiet
Green of clean swept slopes.

Get back! Back off the track!
All (parents, grandparents, and little sisters
Holding _this_ best friend's hand.)

She's coming. The little girl
Who always wins is coming.
Hushed her muffled footbeats.
Part wind. Part sky. A gazelle
Seldom bothering to touch down,
She lifts us in her stride.
Into a harmony that converses
With the clouds. A swan
Discovering she is a swan
She chooses to leave no wake
And disappears beneath a quilt of
Yellow maple leaves hung out to air
Upon their dappled limb.

Off to the side
In the tall grass
And falling leaves
The little brothers play
In tousled tangled pile of boy—
Laughter, sunlight and snaggled tooth.

Get back! Back off the track!
The pack is coming! Our surge of
pounding, elbowing overachievers,
Every mother's precious entry
This herd of red-faced lipbiters.
Pony tails bob in rubber bands.
Budding torsos twist in athletic bras.
Braces gleam in metallic sunlight.
Chunks of white Nike laced in school colors
Pound unmercifully the cringing turf.
For team. For school. For coach. For parents
They run. They run to win.

Off to the side
In the tall grass
The little brothers
Do not look up from their play
To watch the grimaces
Of their sisters run by.

But Liza. Where is Liza?
New-mother-in-town searches
Each straining face for her Liza.
Liza. Who hates her new school
Her new teammates who run off
At practice in twos and threes
Look back at her with snobbish smiles.
Liza, banker's daughter, snatched
From friends in Louisville, Raleigh
And Charlotte and set down
Always in the very best school.

Get back! Back off the track!
It's Liza. Liza's coming. Come on Liza. Catch up!
Liza. One last volley of breath stored in
Tortured lungs where now only knives reside.
Liza stops. And with the roar of a
Wounded beast, explodes
"Breathing. Breathing is important, too."
What did she say? What did that little new girl say?
She said to her mother's face
She said to any scrap of sanity
Left in us all. She said
"Breathing. Breathing is important, too."

Only the little brothers
Playing off to the side
In the tall grass
Paid no heed
Had no need to hear.

The little girl who always wins, wins
And walks off. She wears the arm of
Her coach about her shoulders.
He pushes his words into her ear.

The boys run next. The fathers
Have already started to line up.
They call the little brothers
From their play. To watch.

Wrong Way

The days stumble over each other now.
Pile up at my feet. Good days on
bad days on nothing days.
Parts of them sticking out every which way.
They have no sense of direction.

It's getting to be a real mess.

I want to be introduced to my days properly
at their source. Launch them gently so
they will have a real chance—pastel waterlilies
floating downstream—blooming as they pass.

But these days continue to attack even before
the paper comes—the trash is picked up—
the tops of my pantyhose are dry.
Slip up on me fast. Hit me hard.

Before I know which ramp to take.

Now we *are* in big trouble. All the days
are traveling at breakneck speed. It must
be naptime but I dare not step out
in this traffic.

The Trouble

"The trouble is up *here*," he points out
"between your two ears."
Not out *there*

where life swirls in eternal rush hour
metal scraping metal, riveting brain.
They are revved up now bearing down
on the checkered flag.
Weep weep upon the shoulder
then roll clear into the thistles.
Litter quickly covers.

Hair sticks to the jackhammer
beneath my scalded feet.
Boundaries crumble into polluted seas
and my grandmother's Lady Baltimore cake
falls into pink pieces.

On guard! On guard!
admit only those tattooed
on both buttocks.

The trouble is not out *there*
but up *here* between
my two ears
where eagles lift from tall mountains
and sonatas sweep across still waters.

Tremor

Stuttering head,
hand fluttering, birdlike.
In the end, it is the quiver in the voice
that gives us away
to you
whose eyes lock with mine
coupling over the toasted crust
of *my* club sandwich,
the smooth rim of *your* glass of tea,
the serrated edge of *my* newspaper,
the slick unturned pages of *your* magazine.

Look up
and *there* they are.
Here.   There.   Everywhere.
Those twin white pools
where swim dark pupils
your naked inquisitiveness
plugged into *my* sensitivity.

Has my alter ego abandoned ship
or is it incarcerated below
awaiting arrival in another port?
Perhaps that divinity that stirs in us all
has chosen
to take cover until this life blows over.

I summon my erstwhile self
to come to my defense.
To lift the chin of this convulsive head,
the soles of this slovenly gait.
To get on with it.

Eyeball to eyeball
double dog
dare ye
to look
away.   away.   away
Gotcha!

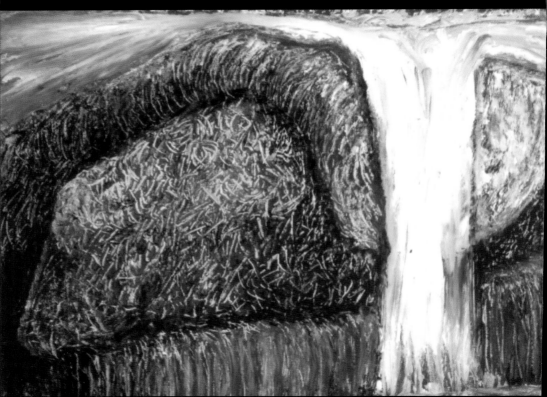

At Times

Come,
Lightning thrust.
Spark
Friction's flame.
Pain
Conceives thought.

How close to the edge
Does one dare creep?
How far bends the twig
Before it breaks?
And opens the floodgates
To the madness that waits
So patiently there and (at times)
Calls my name.

Before

Could you not
hear me
suck up all those feelings
that spilled over inside me?

See me
open my mouth
to let them go free?

Was my call so shrill
that you shut it out?

Next time
I must remember
to press the soft pedal

before
I scream.

Conspiracy

Words conspire against me now
lurk back there—just beyond my grasp
racks and racks of them
computerized responses—my software
labeled appropriate combinations
my great unspoken
punch lines
clever repartee
misplaced names and places
who wait now until
the meeting adjourns
the receiver is hung up
the elevator door closes
the plane takes off
the party is over.

Then
they emerge with a smirk
drag their feet just inside
the entry to my mind
as if they have been there all the time
present their engraved cue card on a silver tray
bowing from the waist.

I grab the ball
go up for the lay-up
but the final buzzer has sounded
the crowd is filing from the arena
I am left hanging on the rim
groping forever in midair
for the word that came to me too late.

Lesser Voices

Those of us who can add
little significance to the
ongoing discussion

push our precious pebbles
to the edge,
reach beyond ourselves
to drop them one by one
into an already voluminous sea
of existing solutions.
Then we retreat to our lair
content to have observed
only the smallest of ripples,
an imperceptible rise
in the level of understanding
a barely discernable
deepening in the lovely clear
blue shade of truth.

Or

We enter the rhetoric
on dry land. Striding, double spaced
under our cover sheet, to slide
beneath the closed door—*sealed*
in a plain manila envelope.

Come back here right now!

Hold still
> for just one more picture and
> don't you dare move a muscle.

Hold still
> for something in your eye
> a splinter in your thumb
> a band-aid on your knee.

Hold still
> please don't twist and turn

> in your seat while you eat.
> I'm pouring milk
> I'm cutting up your meat.

Hold still
> you are forever moving

> when I part your hair
> wipe your nose, wash your ears
> tie your shoe, zip you up.

Hold still
> must you run down the hall
> jump off the sofa
> fight in the living room?

Those are *your good clothes, you know!*

Hold still
> while I get a sponge
> that ice cream cone is dripping
> that grape popsicle is slipping.

Hold Still

Hold still

> for the barber, the dentist, the doctor
> it will only hurt a little, sting a minute
> it won't taste *all* that bad.

> When you look me in the eye
> *hold still,*
> and listen just this once.
> Will you please stop bouncing that ball!

Hold still

> your batteries always charged
> your feet glued to the pedals
> must you forever be going
> > *somewhere else?*

Hold still

> for your goodnight kiss, one last
> glass of water—just one more story
> it's getting much too late.

My heart is just so tired
of chasing you, tugging with you.
Won't you please settle down
and *hold still*.

I am *your Mother, you know!*

I'm just trying to
trying to *hold you here*.
I'm just trying to *hold you*
still.

Spare-a-Dime

"Spare-a-dime, Spare-a-dime
Gonna get drunk another time."

Our hands about our mouths,
we hobbled. One foot in the gutter.
Mocked him. Followed him, clear
to the church corner. White sashes
from our pinafores dragged dust.

"Spare-a-dime, Spare-a-dime
Gonna get drunk another time."

Crooked wisp of a black man
Spare-a-Dime paid us no never mind.
Whiskers. Scraggly white hair
bobbed about his tottering head.
like a misplaced halo.
Pants cuffs shredded down a thousand sidewalks.
Mismatched shoes. Someone else's blisters inside.

"You all come back here!
Spare-a-Dime don't need no
younguns pestering his day.
Anyways, ain't fitting."
Mai Carter leaned on her broom
"Lord knows the times
Mama and Papa left us sitting
in that wagon. Saturday on Main Street.
Waiting for him to come to town.

Robert McLemore was his name then.
On a high school diploma, too.
And Lord, them silk suits from St. Louis
measured just for him. Felt hats,
soft and white as a new lamb.
Shoes from Burke's in Nashville.
Ummm-ummph! We was proud.
Set up high. Seen him open the bank.
Big brass knob. Slow. Easy like.

Mr. McLemore used front doors
when he went in and black folks
spoke to him like he was white folks.
A professional, Papa said.
A black barber in the white barbershop.
Front chair. Judges and sheriffs and
all the bank mens went to him and
he knowed things no other black man
heard tell of and they tipped their hats
to him on the street.

And Robert McLemore went to war
with them but what he seen out there
in France be so bad for him that
Robert McLemore never lift his eyes again.
And Spare-a-Dime, he don't. He don't ask
for nothing but a dime and Mama says
mens give him all they dimes so he
can be 'shamed for them."

Mai Carter shook the dust from our sashes
slid the pinafore ruffles back in place
swiped both chastised bottoms at once.
"Go on now. Mind your manners."

"Spare-a-dime, Spare-a-dime
Gonna get drunk another time."

She and I

were friends at four
at twelve and twenty
at sixty and more.

I knew her freckles
with buttermilk
on them

(and wanted them too
if you
must know.)

She and I

She learned
to ride
on my bicycle

and held me up
while I
learned to skate.

Judy always
waited at the corner
for me

and I always
waited there
for her.

She drove me
when I was afraid
to drive

(she knew
but never ever
told.)

I went
when her husband
died. . . .

She came
when my daughters
married. . . .

Judy and I
built stick houses
in the mud

for our china dolls.

"It's got cancer.
The whole place has cancer.
It's spreading faster 'n the two of us can handle
the rust and rot and leaks."

"I've got to carry it on,"
I had said when he died.
"We can't sell his way of life.
Our grandchildren would never know."
And we took it, the homeplace.
So their Sunday dinners would have real ice cream
and just-picked green beans . . . fried country ham.
So they'd eat honey from the hives
and grind wheat for their bread.

But money went to schools and cars.
And Clara and Clint and Shorty
and Maceo and Hannah Mai
had to go one by one until only Clara came
one day a week and then not at all.
The oaks had grown too tall
the preserving power of sun
gave way to corrupting shadow of shade
and the wood rot started slowly
under doorsills and in low corners
and what you put back
cost twice as much. Was only half as good.

It crumbled powdery in your hands. The rot.
So we took down the observatory
where we climbed aloft to see the stars.
And the second story of the treehouse
where all the good danger was.
And the catwalk from the transplanted caboose
where we lay on our backs. Told tales of far-off places.

Homeplace

We fought the rust, too, on red tin roofs
putting on paint that lasted a year and
patching with tar that didn't sound
anywhere near as good in the rain.
And the cupolas went from the barn.
Pigeons had roosted there too long.

We washed everything in Clorox
and painted with special paint that
took vacation money but
the lattice work on the gazebo slid into crazy patterns
and we stained Ma's tea table to cover
the new bad words someone else's children
must've learned from television.

"Let it go," my tired bones cried at night.
"It's not the same. Times are different.
We can't hold it together."
But *he* never said it
Tho' his Saturdays split rails
and propped up leaning posts
put new boards in the bridge
new pipes in the cattle gaps.

Sometimes when the dishes were done
we sat on the front porch in the cool of dark
and listened to a calf answering his mother
across the big field.
And talked about next Sunday
when they would all come out
to dig sweet potatoes and walk the woods
to play ball and talk old times.
Then we'd hold hands
and not really mind too much
that we were spending ourselves
to buy time to ease the pain—the passing
of a dying way.

Aunt Willie

It's a good thing I shall be light.
Not six men left
could call my name
much less carry my box up Poker Hill.
My world was full of men—
men dancing with me waving to me winking
wagonloads of men Main Street full of men
doctors bankers lawyers grocers
"Iceman, Miss Willie" at my back door
preachermen old preachers young preachers
at my wedding in my pulpit at my table.
Men my men my world
all gone.
Only I
growing smaller until no one will guess
that the pea is under the eggshell.
Oh! but there is more to come
I've seen the stages
through the half-opened doors down the hall.
One lying entwined in bed bars
like a spider falling from his web.
One moaning in unknown tongues
from her life before.
One tied. One gasping.
Shall they all be me, Lord?
Do you need me to wait while you tidy up
or is the gate so small
that I must come bit by bit
whittled down until I fit?
I grow smaller, Lord.
I grow smaller
with each leftover year.

On Her List

A friend
stopped by today
on her way to aerobics
bringing her Aunt Sarah's potato salad.
We made room in the refrigerator
and talked of the nice day we were having.
When she left
I put her name
on the Food List
and went in to lie back down.

Now
my friend
won't have to come to the funeral
if it should be bad that day
or she can't find anyone to come with
or she has already accepted something
that she can't possibly decline
at the last minute.

Now
my friend
is checking my name off
the things-to-do list
she keeps on the front seat
and her family can have the leftover
potato salad for dinner.

Aunt Sarah's potato salad is foolproof.

Daisy Field

Daisies wilt a little each day
When there is nothing left for them to say

When they have tickled bellies of newborn calves
And beckoned lovers along garden paths

Hidden in corners behind tall grass
Raced up to the highway to feel cars whiz past

Preened reflections in the creek
Taken sun and rain bloomed past their peak

Then daisies wilt a little each day
For there is nothing left for them to say

Theirs is a small life—in a large field they grow
It is the same with daisies and most everyone I know.

Always Before This Summer

I do not hear a call to the podium.
I am not the poet of this summer.

I sing of tall dark corn
filled out and tasseled
crowding single file into chosen fields.
Of succulent stems that snap
and generous pastureland
rolled up in great round bales.
Of lazy laughing summers meandering
to nowhere in particular.

I am not the bard
of this imposter
who fries our days
and tosses them one upon another
cow chips stacked
in the hot metal bed of a pick-up.
Who squeezes from the creases of night
that last hoping and leaves it limp
wrung out.
Sentencing its creatures
to empty wandering searches
scrawny coats. Castigated indignity.

I find no voice
for an impotent earth staring crazed
into the white heat of a nothing sky
teeth clinched in protracted agony
beneath stubble singed to final brown.

I strain instead
with the red rimmed eyes of the farmer
who abandons his tractor in midfield.
Succumbs to swirling dust fine as face powder,
death mask of the vanishing topsoil
nurtured with his days and nights
held to his breast, spewed with his sweat,
and now drips with dry white tears
of surrender.

How much do I hear for one ordinary neighbor?
What will you give me for
his pride his youth his dream?
Wagered in one lifelong crap game.
Gambling that it would rain eventually.
Because it always had before.
Always before this summer.

Fourth of July

The ground is always hard
beneath the spread
of Fourth of July quilts.

And the wait is always
a little longer
than children want to wait.

So they lay back and look up
cupping shaggy heads
in stubby laced fingers,

crossing browned legs
to jiggle a white sneaker
anxiously in the air.

Wish away the daylight
that dawdles now
at compressing its spent color

into floating stripes of rose pink
then tucks them away
behind the hills.

Together, we wait for this reluctant
night to pull a black canopy
up around her neck then

cannons roar and soar and streak!
A thousand mouths gape
in open wonder as if on cue.

Earth quivers innards quake heavens burst
and run down the face of sky.
We have duly impregnated this summer
with celebration.

Our flag, drawn in burning embers,
is seared into the night.
Applause crisply contagiously ripples
some whistle through their teeth.
This Fourth of July fizzles and goes out.
Dark erases all mention of our intrusion.

Mothers meticulously fold their quilts.
Children take their fathers' hands, fan out
collecting little family groups.

Drawn by unerring magnets to front stoops
they turn to stare back into the empty night
searching for the faces of their lost brothers

who must forever come to pay the cost
of our independence,
our Fourth of July.

Table for Two by the Window

The one in the yellow straw hat
is seated with her back to me.
The shoulder pads of her sky-blue linen
suit square up precisely with the
yellow diamonds on the damask of the
french chair. Her hands tremble when she
reaches to butter the hard roll. It
crumbles from the force of the silver
butter knife. She abandons both.
Shaking her hands. Wiping them on
her linen napkin. Her speech is
relentless. Her head jerks
with the propulsion of each word. She
leaves no pause for a return
volley by her younger opponent.

I can see her. Full face. Black.
She is all in black. The Egyptian
necklace occasionally disappears
into her blouse. Her hands fumble
to bring it out again but her eyes
remain riveted to the face, the mouth
that moves below the yellow hat as
if her words were plotting to escape,
never to be heard from again. They enter
instead the steel trap of her companion's
unblinking gaze. Her eyes swallow them.
She digs her unpainted nails into the table's edge
leaving two perfect rows of half-moons imprinted
on the white cloth. Through the window
the caution light blinks yellow. yellow. yellow.
Slashes yellow across their faces,
their unresolved desperation,
their silver spoons of crème brûlée.

The Newspaper

Each morning
the cool grey dream
of the sidewalk
is shattered
when *yesterday* is delivered—
rolled up in rainproof plastic
slapped hard across
its sleeping face.

It scarcely leaves a mark—
no lasting impression.
It is not even *news*
to the sidewalk.
It has heard it *all*
from the night before
through the open windows,
between the lace curtains
caught hanging out.

The sidewalk has *felt*
the sting of footsteps
in running pursuit, *felt*
live screams grate down its spine
outwailing the sirens
speeding to on-the-spot terror
screeching to up-to-the-minute bloodshed.

Neon runs red
Through the EXIT sign.
Blood through my brain
When traffic jams
Temporarily dislodge.

We seekers converge in orderly fashion.
The price is reduced for senior citizens.
Most have paid their own way.

Exit

Outside, some wait in line just to get in.
Our seats will stay warm for the next performance.

On stage, the old juggler tosses his pins too high.
He reaches in three directions at once.

My feet walk themselves toward the familiar.
The sunlight is turned all the way up to HIGH.
I shield my squinting eyes.

Waiting beneath its bush
The golden egg has spoiled.
I stoop to pick it up
It oozes between my fingers.
There is another.

I bumble on.
Laugh at small things.
Pick up pebbles in the stream
To feel.

Perennials

I slid across the top rail of the fence
worn slick to pink wood with my crossings.
Time to pull the stakes of the garden.
The weeds had grown waist high
and I would be glad when the tobacco was in
then Copperhead would come with the mower
to wipe clean the field that had fed my family—
and would for awhile from the freezer and the pantry.

As the dew squished in on my tennis shoes
I gathered the last of the crowder peas
and tugged at a few fat stubby carrots
and thought of the summer that had been—

Of you in your gardens
pulling up stakes and moving pots inside
committing happy times to memory
relegating tense moments to family jokes.
I thought of all the hours the Lord and I
had pulled weeds here together
to weather the storms inside me.
And I began to realize
as I said goodbye to all around me
the black butterfly on the red zinnia
the brittle cornstalk ready for compost—
that the asparagus, strawberry, and I
would be the sole survivors of winter's charge.
God's perennials
providing continuity
and promise. Hope.

Time to Dig

the world stares
but dares not speak

there's time to dig
as a white dog digs

discarding the mounds
between my hind legs

down to emptiness
I look around
for a bone
to bury

here.

Seventeen

The thick oak door slammed twice behind him.
The white Nova reared reeled
screamed from the gate.

That night words had not been words at all
but darts pulled from sheathes of despair
aimed into flesh rubbed raw by probing.

I turned out the lights and went on upstairs.

Apron strings when severed too quickly . . .
bleed from both ends.

They're selling their things today.
At auction.
The frail little Franklin sisters
won't be there.

They no longer count the collection
in the Presbyterian church vestibule
every Sunday. Or take their walk
at three o'clock every afternoon—
in long black coats
a red felt hat and a blue
Miss Lollie's hand on Miss Alice's arm.

They've moved them out now
to the Harpeth Terrace Nursing Home.
The church gave them a lovely reception.
But they weren't there either.
They never did approve of serving refreshments
at the church . . . still don't.

Every afternoon now
at the nursing home
they put on their long black coats
the red hat and the blue
and pack shopping bags for home.
Then one or the other whispers
"Sister, they've been so lovely to us today.
It would be such a shame to hurt their feelings.
Shouldn't we just stay this night?"
And they hang up their coats
and their hats.

Franklin Sisters

They're selling their things today.
The frail little Franklin sisters.
August 12, 10:00 A.M.
House built 1810.
A wood stove.
An oak bowfront china press.
Hundreds of items not mentioned.
Lunch served on the grounds.
Something desirable for everyone.
Cash on day of sale.

Assisted Living

The old women are getting ready.
They have all they can do
Just emptying those bags of anger.

But the old men—
Their dreams do not understand
This ending.

So they wander.
Follow Brenda
Room to room.
Hold to the mop handle
In her cleaning cart.
And search for the door
They came out of.

Olive Trees

Here He fell upon His face
where branches bend to earth

"Oh my Father, if it be possible. . . ."

Gnarled and twisted they rise
forever dipped in moonlight
lifted leaves shimmer

whisper still
if any would but listen.

"Not as I will—as Thou wilt."

Gethsemane, Gethsemane
drink from thine own cup
olive trees restoreth themselves
and live on

behind an open gate.

Desert Dark Child

Desert dark child
running knotted joints
toward speeding tourist bus,
drawn as a gnat
to twin beams of light.

Desert dark child,
trailing red tatters
from your slender mast,
bleeding purpled shadow
lengthened to absurdity,
into still warm sands.
Stretching spindly fingers
to gather to your tiny breasts
bouquets of cascading nothingness.

Desert dark child
I hear the silence of your futile cry
mimic echoes of this barrenness.
I feel the frailty of your dirty fingernails
scrape deep trenches across my hollow heart.
My desert dark child.

Wailing Wall

I carried your name to the wall . . . coiled
with the others . . . a spring . . . in the catacombs
of my brain . . . over continents . . . through
customs . . . the Zion Gate . . . down stone alleys . . .
Herod's walled city . . . Via Dolorosa . . . past excavation . . .
crumbling cup . . . brittle bone . . . Great Portico . . .
approach to . . . Solomon's Temple . . . colossal
columns . . . defying the viewfinder . . . the Dung Gate . . .
I confront . . . the Wailing Wall

On the men's side   On the women's side
beyond barbed wire   I approach. A bride
orthodox flutter   fearfully holding my father's
coattails flap.   freckled arm
Blackbirds fly   eyes glued to the altar
in to roost.   my single stone
Topknots bob.   magnified, menacing
Peck prayers into stone.   baseboard to my faith.

Nineteen stones below Jesus stood.
Walked. Cleared the Temple.
My life gushes before me. Recedes.
Tidal wave splashing stone.
The past falls from my fingertips
A forgotten toy, released. Clangs to pavement.
Names come reluctantly. Tin scraped
from tongue into impervious stone.

Why are you here? What did you bring?
asks the Wall. . . . No exit sign. No detour
arrow. This is *the* ultimate wall. Pitted
centuries. Crevices crammed. Thin rolled prayer . . .
petitions . . . reminders *to* God of his promises.

At my side other tongues taste tears.
  One rocks. Stretches an embroidered apron
    across bloated belly.
  One paces. Stringy ringlets drip sweat
          down dusty boots . . . into cobblestone.

Now. Now your names ring as chimes . . .
coming in clearly . . . your *own* voices . . . from
nursing homes . . . tennis courts . . . Krogers . . .
supper tables . . . I listen . . . *you* call *your* name . . .
others I had forgotten. . . . *You* stand beside
me . . . behind me. . . . No longer afraid . . . not
alone in my faith. . . . The stone no barrier now
advances . . . taking me in. . . . Suspended there . . .
tightly. Tenderly held . . . I leave your name inside.

Desert Rendezvous

Steward of the Sinai
lone upright
squared in regal stance
silent surveyor of
these ancient sands
shifting capsules of recorded time
embers of
crystallized bone and stone
petrified thought.

Which of our gods divined this rendezvous
discreetly erasing your trail of footsteps
far from the rusting tin and rotting twine
of your Bedouin hut

from straggling sheep
hobbled donkey
tethered camel?

O shepherd of stillness
faceless ripple upon long ago sea
interceptor of intercontinental flight
pilgrim tourists
encased in Egyptian caravan
bussed from alien borders
blinking into your velvet dusk
our glaring headlights' intrusion.

Fore and aft your dark young camouflaged ride
guns across their knees
together we glide upon sculptured surfaces
as purpled rays finger rising swells
pierce concaveness
carousing each gilt-edged cavern
forever seeking to ferret
infinite treasure
from the unknown.

To what horizon do you lift your shadowed gaze?
Where melds this blanket of sand
this blur of sky for you?
Do you too read these settling patterns
as gaping ribs of time
littered with unfinished fantasies
strewn with defeated dreams
lying like abandoned wounded
reaching, crying for their missing parts?

Or is it only peace you gather in your gaze
inhaling stark simplicity from your scope
excluding the world's excesses exploding
far beyond the grasp of your veil?

My solitary sentinel
along what shores will the waves of our thought lap
across what desert floors will they blow distilled
when shall we sink into our separate turfs
unaware of horizons we have left unclaimed?

Space

My eyes penetrate your gaze
I feel your gaze invade my eyes

and upon that fragile intervening field
where dwells the dignity of our separateness

our love is written.

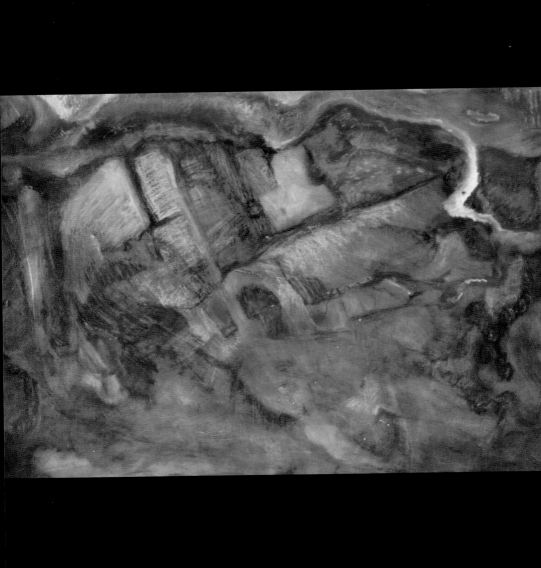

The Land Waited

The land waited peaceful and whole.
The Indian came
to hunt plentiful small game
deer and bear
to camp in the shadows of the large beech grove
that stood between here
and the river
to fish clear streams
drink from sweet springs.

The land waited peaceful and whole.
The settler came
from Virginia across mountains
on horseback in covered wagon
his name was Perkins
and he carried with him
a Revolutionary War grant
title to this land
and as far as you can see
came to clear his land
to fell the beech trees
to split these handsome logs
that would shelter his hearth
and protect his kin.

The farmer came
to till with hoe to plow by hand
this rich bottom land
that would grow tall corn
and ripen full grain
to fence fields for
whitefaced cattle sheep hogs
red mules grey percheron horses
to build barns on cut-stone foundations
looming over the countryside so fine
that townspeople rode out in black buggies
just to see them
the farmers were named Yankee Smith Hamilton
Green Price Griggs Bass and Murrey
Sims and Sawyer.

When the tractor came
they grew new crops for feed
lespedeza alfalfa soybeans
their neighbors came
from seven adjoining farms
to thrash the grain
to put up the hay
to kill the hogs
to eat the spreads
their wives fixed at noon
and in the worst of droughts
to quench their thirst
and that of their stock
to survive upon
these indomitable springs.

Fieldstone Farms came
to plan with integrity and infinite care
to carve out compatible pools
playgrounds walking trails
and to build.

Now you come
to raise families
to plant your vegetables and flowers
to canoe and fish these streams
to stand with Indian settler and farmer
at eventide
watching fiery sunsets
ignite these purple hills
letting the peace of this place
imbue your souls
its vitality propel your lives
and perhaps at times to run your hands
along these time-worn logs
to feel the pain and pride
of him who split and raised them
the abundance of life
they have since absorbed.

These logs these lands are your legacy
bequeathed in remembrance of those
who invested their lives here
tend them carefully and with reverence
for there will be others
yet to come.

—Given on the occasion of the dedication of the Sims Room
in the Clubhouse at Fieldstone Farms,
April 1993.

Laureats

The hills have no need for a poet.
They have always been their own.
Their poets *are* whereof they speak.
Know by heart the lay of the land.
Have it memorized inside out.

They recite with chests bared.
Shout at sky jagged outcroppings
of limestone layers, then softly
render pastorals to soothe eroding
slopes with sponges of textured moss.

And they read very well—with authority
citing ancestral terrains—testimonials
from glaciers that ravaged then birthed
in catastrophic shifts, that wake even now
echoes of upheaval to rumble in their bowels.

What poetic license gives me, a mortal voice
trembling, naked at their feet, claim
to kinship before this sitting court of kings
this royal clan whose voices stride about the countryside
in jeweled metaphor of silver stream,
in bronzed image of field?

At sunset when the hills melt
into their soft-hearted rose refrain
and lean to robe us in the ethereal shade
of all-forgiving shadow,
which whispers from my lips can challenge
the eloquence of their noble faces
chiseled from the bedrock of truth
to crown the landscape of my heart?

Through the Sunset

sing
u
lar
ly
the sure
round
notes

Chopin

float
d
o
w
n

gilt-edged
through
the sunset

translucent
truth
clarity
in
all colors

t	t	t
u	u	u
r	r	r
n	n	n
i	i	i
n	n	n
g	g	g

to settle
one
upon
another
into
our thirsting
upturned
lives

Oh! Miss Lizzie, what long ago harp echoes
in the deepest corner of my heart
as your fingers play once more
across this rich tapestry of your years?

It became today "Our Family Quilt."
We chose it first, Miss Lizzie,
when we divided up *their things.*

All lovely in your life bequeathed
in precious fragments of fabric—
days spinning sunshine on striped parasols
down wide even vistas. Brick paths.
Nights rustling taffeta, trailing ball gowns,
sashes of crisp ribbon. Brocade from your window seat.
Delicate swatches, cream-colored silk . . . lace
turned back upon your waiting bed.

Not one dark remnant from the plagues
that early orphaned you and
waited upon your every threshold.
Instead, a yellow pansy painted
into a square of black velvet
featherstitched bound in gold.
No tattered blue or grey. Fallen lieutenants
stolen from your life and country.
Instead, a crimson star, satinstitched on grey silk
wreathed in federal blue.
No hint of empty cupboard, endless bedside vigil.
Instead, a length of coral silk, a briarstitched
diamond, pale lavender hue.

I tuck the deep red backing between the walnut spools.
Retrace your chainstitched name across one corner
and lean to gentle those softest of blue velvets
against my cheek.

We chose much more than your quilt
for our family, Miss Lizzie.
Today, we chose you.

Mountainscape

Mountains rise . . . then rise again
granite swells dashed onto flatness
muscular shoulders
rub . . . jostle for position
push-pull shapes opposed
projected lines extended
mammoths spawn mammoths
then recede . . . fade into sky
shifting stones rumble bowels
constrained forces pulsate surface
veils of transparency float in
to layer
smother
shield
until lifted gently at their corners
reveal their breathless exposé

sunlight sweeps in random searches
focuses absently, fingers textures
then abruptly turns fickle

shadow leaks black ink into puckered seams
flattens blends blurs
one into another
until a single silhouette
runs dark against sky
hung there for those who sit
at the base of monuments
to weep.

Struggle

The thing is the struggle.
The getting a grip on.
A hold comes easily
then twists away.
The forces on down the line
whip it from you
spinning it out of control
flinging you about . . . off course.

But if you can get a leg over
you can climb on top
and your weight will be an advantage.

Getting on top
is the thing.
Then just riding this life out.

The Pleasure of Reordering

It is an awesome thing
watching God undo a summer.
Shedding density. Pruning lushness.
Folding greens into reds
yellows into bronze
drying succulent crisp.
Putting away. Taking down. Clearing.
But without the regret
the looking back. The grief
with which we move reluctantly
from one phase of life to another.

Rather all is accomplished
with heightened awareness.
Brimming expectation.
We feel it in the first crackle.
of leaves, underfoot. See it in vibrancy
of color descending one leaf at a time
from the top of the dogwood.
Find it in tinges of lavender
creeping into divesting woods.
Sure sign of faith
that tomorrow can be lovelier
than the loveliest today.

God must revel in the joy of change
the pleasure of reordering.
In summer's last zinnia blooming
next to fall's first chrysanthemum.
In crab apples so carefully hung above
pokeberries running wild on red stems.
In the fat green mock orange that thuds
to the ground. Rolls downhill. Right at
the fox-tail squirrel that looks around.
Takes a bite and skitters
back up the same tree.

Wind in the Cedars

The cedars stand waiting along the rail fence
huddled in twos and threes
still, silent, straight.
Timid girls.

The wind strides across the bare meadows
up from the river in
mounting urgency.

The waiting cedars bend. Bend with the wind
gently at first and now in pulsing rhythm
as toying, tempting, teasing
they are caught, released and caught again
spines arched in each embrace.

Lifting green gowns of linen and velvet
sifting summer's dust from dainty lacework
the wind snaps clean the last weak twigs
reaches in to inhale fragrance from their bosoms.
Lets go and turns
to swagger up the hill toward the mighty oaks.

Father, We Are at the Morning Now

Father, we are at the morning now
when life begins to change color
and shed that which budded and blossomed
once in us
shading and sheltering our own
through the summer of our lives.

Now bared against the horizon
stand we as we are. Unadorned—
pretense spread about our feet.
Deeper rooted.
Pruned by seasons past.

We face this winter's wind
waiting on our hillsides. Unattended—
parents depart, children move away.
We pray aloud or in whispers as we choose.

Unencumbered—we respond
to the very breath of God.

Father, we are at the morning now.
Walk with us through the dew.

October

October nestles her warm purr between my breasts
and sends a playful paw swatting
at the chill on the tip of my nose.

She lolls at noon beneath a sky infinitely bluer
than any blue has a right to be
seductively preening her voluptuous calico.

October pounces upon an unsuspecting world

and having tossed it around a bit
leaves with a satisfied smile.

That
Fox

We saw the fox this morning.
There's one thing about that fox,
he knows who he is. And he
knows where he's going,
setting out from his den
on the other side of the hill.

He sticks that nose out front
shrubby tail flagging behind him
little legs whipping under him
fast short even little steps
making time—heading to the river.
Sighting down
that sharp pointy nose—
a diagonal
across wide winter fields.

I surprised him once
coming down the gravel road.
He didn't miss a beat.
Just cut a wide circle around me,
never batted an eye.
Nose still pointed to the river.

Comes back the same way,
up the hill fast little fox-steps,
satisfied, secretive
smiling to himself.
You can almost hear him humming.

Not that we see him that often,
four times this past year
that I can remember.
Once in the snow
he just came and sat in the side yard
his red-orange coat fluffed out
white ascot ruffed under his chin
head up sniffing cold . . . superior
like this white carpet had been rolled out
just for him and he had come,
was here to take charge.

Last summer in the worst of droughts
he came in broad daylight
to the cats' pans
right up against the house.
Walking sideways, mangy looking,
half-starved, embarrassed like
he hated coming ragged and dirty.
Begging us to look the other way.
Slinked off close to the ground.
I could have cried.

Foxes take poorly to humbling.

That's why we're so glad
to see him this morning.
We run from window to window
watch him clear out of sight.
Prissing across that field.
Skimming over that frost.
Just look at him—
he's something else today.

That fox.
Pointy little nose
stuck way out front
heading to the river.

Three Good Questions for October

1. How does the God
   of lovely seasons
       who speaks to us today
       from temples of yellow maple
   speak to the terrorist
       brooding in his back alley?

2. Where does the God
   of everyman
       who walks with us this day
       along cedar-scented corridors
   walk with him
       who carries a bomb?

3. How may we
       as worshipers at an altar
       of love and forgiveness
   press a yellow maple leaf
       into his powder-burned hand?

Passes on Through

I *do* know that river birch leaves
turning yellow, have no voice. Cannot sing.
Yet I can most assuredly tell you that
I do distinctly hear their round notes
sound when the gentlest of fall showers begin.

A scale. A tender string of leaves
laced upon a limb. Scored against the dark hum
of cedars. First this leaf flicked, then that,
then the two, as cymbals ring. A stir.
A ping of delicate lavenders lifted upon a breeze

comes and goes until mustering enough
force to move on up the bank
and call its full-fledged orchestra into play—
slickening the barn path, greying the white stone
at the back door, then whirling around the far corner,
it passes on through. Leaves only the yellow song
of the river birch running down the window panes,
thumping at the eves. Winter coming on.

– Francis Scott Key

**DISABLED AMERICAN
VETERANS**
Cincinnati, Ohio 45250-0301
www.dav.org

God sent out the invitations
To that first Thanksgiving.
You see He spoke both
Indian and Pilgrim.
He invited us to this one, too.
He always includes
The Indians
And the Pilgrims.
And because everyone knows
Thanksgiving would never work
Unless it was Indian . . . Pilgrim . . .
Indian . . . Pilgrim . . . Indian . . . Pilgrim
He has place cards.
So all the Indians won't sit together
And all the Pilgrims won't sit together.

For openers
There's the blessing.
It had been a hard year that first Thanksgiving
And before this one, too,
And all the others in between, for that matter.
Life is hard.
So we never have any trouble
Being thankful just to be included.
We really do appreciate
All He has done for us.
And it feels good to tell Him so.

After the blessing we share
Whatever extra we have gotten out of life
That someone else might need some more of
On their plate today.

Some happy souls have brought laughter
Big bunches of long-stemmed laughter.
Some others have brought interest
Real homegrown 100% interest.
Encouragement.
There's a whole platter of family recipes
For encouragement and inspiration.
That downhome fired-up kind of inspiration.
Ideas—there are never enough ideas to go around.
And peace and quiet
Are both in short supply and great demand.
But there's love—lots of love
Enough for everyone to have seconds.

Some folks bring plenty
But have a hard time taking.
And they go home with empty baskets and hearts.
And some don't bother to bring much of anything
They go home loaded—but still hungry
For the joy of giving.
But others come wagging everything they have.
And help themselves bountifully to everything
Everyone else has brought.
And on the way home they remark
That each year it gets harder to tell
The Indians from the Pilgrims
(Without their nametags).
They *all* are beginning
To look so much like
Their Father.

The Otherside

It is the wind that changes
blowing us this way then that
just as we get set in our minds.

It is the wind that changes
east across the hills
then swirling in from the north
to reshuffle the settling leaves
rolling them over backwards
exposing truths we didn't know
were there.

It is the wind that changes
else we would never ever see
the otherside of things.

The Yellow Flowers

They are always the last to leave.
"Goodbye. Goodbye."   The yellow flowers
Have come up to say "Goodbye."

Erase the golden streaks that raced across
The billowing skirts of unkept fields.

Fade the dancing sparklers, that fizzle and
Go out upon the brown apron of the woods lot.

The yellow flowers totter to the roadside shoulder now.
Lean. Unsteady on those stilted sun-dried stems.

Those clusters of cherub faces, button cheeks,
Tramp through the lavender crush of underbrush.

Pendulums joined at the root sweeping
To the edge—glancing over their shoulders.

Swing back choked aghast at the poisoned breath
Of traffic, the savage whispering of speed.

With bronzed tassels they futilely flag
Our blank unseeing stare. Our urgency.

Upstaging our coming with their going.
They smear our windshield, our dark distracted eye

With the final powdery pollen of their brilliance.
It is we who disappear and leave no trace.

Our Flight

A white butterfly
undoes its wings
against the weathered wood
of the porch railing.
Lays them out flat
on the cool mist
of first light.

Clasp and unclasp
two praying hands
morning's rebirth
of all living things
reaffirmation of
lifelong addiction
to this time. This place.

From temple eves
wild birds sing
crickets call,
our world
inscribes its praise
across the white velvet
of butterfly wings.

Until a clearing is spied
ahead and beyond

our new space

book our flight
on white butterfly wings.

Church
We are listening.
Your old people are listening.
What we hear is Holy Spirit
Rising in voices of our young.
They have danced us down these aisles
To worship at an altar built of praise.

Church
We are watching.
Grandmothers, Grandfathers watching
What we see is faith.
New faith. Bright. Shining.
Lit by The Light. Lifted by The Word.
Learning. Living. Laughing.

Church
Old ones are praying.
Do you hear soft voices praying?
New words. New hymns. New prayers.
Tender thoughts from growing hearts
that speak to tired hearts too.

Church
Reach out!
Wrap your arms around them.
They are heirs to all that we believe.
Call out the name of Jesus.
Watch His answer spread
Across each fresh and trusting face.

Young People
We are following,
Following right behind you.
Go slowly. The oldest are coming too.
Hold our hands. Lead our hearts.
Up these aisles. Out these doors.
Into your street. We want to meet—
This Jesus that you know.

Oh yes, Church, you may follow too.

Fa

jE F
Fatio, Louise.
The Happy Lion's
    treasure. Pictures b...

D1162209

CHILDREN'S LIBRARY
MAIN

DENVER
PUBLIC LIBRARY

FINE FOR OVERTIME

RO1107 09576

THE HAPPY LION'S TREASURE

Also by Louise Fatio and illustrated by Roger Duvoisin

THE HAPPY LION

THE HAPPY LION IN AFRICA

THE HAPPY LION ROARS

THE THREE HAPPY LIONS

THE HAPPY LION'S QUEST

THE HAPPY LION AND THE BEAR

THE HAPPY LION'S VACATION

A DOLL FOR MARIE

RED BANTAM

THE HAPPY LION'S TREASURE

by

Louise Fatio—pictures by Roger Duvoisin

DENVER
PUBLIC LIBRARY
OCT 1971
CITY & COUNTY OF DENVER

McGRAW-HILL BOOK COMPANY

New York • Toronto • London • Sydney
St. Louis • San Francisco • Mexico • Panama

G197362

RO1107 09576

To Jeanne

THE HAPPY LION'S TREASURE
1970 Louise Fatio and Roger Duvoisin. All rights reserved under Berne and Pan-American Copyright Conventions. Reproductions in whole or in part of any portion of the text or any of the illustrations without permission is prohibited. Illustrated by Roger Duvoisin. Simultaneous publication in Canada 1970. Printed in Belgium.
Library of Congress Catalog Card Number: 72-114446

jE F
Fatio, Louise.
The Happy Lion's
   treasure. Pictures b...

It was a cool, spring morning.
Some friends of the Happy Lion had come to his rock garden to chat or to rest cosily against him to be warm and comfortable.

"Happy Lion," said the squirrel, "why don't you make a will?
I have often heard around town that rich and famous people do
make wills."

"That's true," said the pigeon. "And *you are* rich and famous.
Why, last Sunday in the park I heard a lady say to another,
"Our dear Happy Lion has such a rich life. He loves everyone
and everyone loves him. He is famous."

"What's a will?" asked the Happy Lion.

"Something you write into," said a sparrow. "I know that much."

"You don't know much," said a mouse. "I go around town lots more than you do. Into houses, cupboards, closets, into books and drawers. I have seen many wills in my life. I've even tasted a few. And I can tell you, they are not as good as cheese."

"How interesting," laughed a raven. "A will, my friends, is a paper into which all the things that are yours are written down. And it tells to whom you will give them when you grow very, very old, lose your feathers, and die. My ancestors were lawyers. That's how I know."

When the Happy Lion was alone with his lioness, he thought of his little house where swallows built their nests;

he thought of his garden where violets bloomed in the shade of the rocks;

he thought of his moat where the frogs sang at night;

he thought of his two trees where the squirrels and the birds came to sit to talk about the news; and he thought it would be nice to put down all these riches into a will. He had many things to give, indeed.

"Oh, let's make a will," said the lioness. "It will be fun."
"To begin," said the Happy Lion, "let's talk about our moat.
Wouldn't the seal love it! Poor thing, he can hardly dive and
turn around in his tiny pool."
"Have you thought," asked the lioness, "how the seal will carry
the moat to his place? With a watering can, I suppose."

"Well, we'll talk about it later, then."
"We might talk now about our two trees," said the lioness.
"Wouldn't they be just right for the monkey's acrobatics?"

"Yes," agreed the Happy Lion," but only one tree, and NOT the
tree where the owl makes her nest every spring.   That one
should be left for her and for all the birds and squirrels who
need a place to sit and gossip.   But now, we ought to say something about our rocks.   I say the bear should take the biggest
one to climb on and look at Sunday visitors from above."

The two lions did not know that they were not alone in their garden. There was also François, the zookeeper's son and the Happy Lion's best friend. He had walked in quietly to pay a visit. And then there was the raven, still up in the tree. Both had heard the lions' talk.

"May I please interrupt," interrupted the raven. "My ancestors were lawyers as you know; that's why I will say that you cannot put into a will the things that aren't yours."

"OUR house, OUR garden, OUR moat, OUR trees aren't OURS?" cried the lioness.

"They belong to the zoo which belongs to the park which belongs to the city," said the raven.

"Then I have nothing?" exclaimed the Happy Lion. "Nothing to put into my will for my friends? NOTHING?"

"Don't be sad, my Happy Lion," said François, placing his hand on the lion's mane. You have something else to give which is much more precious than two trees, a moat, a rock garden, and a house. You have a very, very, great treasure to put into your will to make all your friends and everybody else happy, in the zoo, in town, and everywhere."

"I have?" asked the Happy Lion.

"He has?" asked the lioness.

"Where?" asked the raven.

"Ah, that is a secret," said François. "I will tell you some day."

"I have a secret treasure?" repeated the Happy Lion with great astonishment when François departed.

"Well," said the raven, "my ancestors were lawyers, as is well known, but all I can say is, I am nonplussed." And he flew off to tell the news to everyone in the park.

It was not long before many of the lion's friends gathered in the rock garden. Even the bear, the Peking duck, the hippopotamus, and the rabbit came.

"Can anyone guess where the secret treasure is?" asked the raven, sitting on the highest rock.

"It's not in my *house*. That I know," said the Happy Lion.

"Then it's under it, that's obvious," said the bear.

"Let me take a look," said the mouse. "I know my way under that house." He disappeared into a hole near the door while the animals gathered around it to watch for him to come out.

He was away a long time. When he finally reappeared at the corner of the house, the Happy Lion asked,

"Have you found anything?"

"Nothing. Nothing but ants, cockroaches, and spiders."

"It's evidently under the big rocks," assured the robin. "That's where *I* would bury a treasure."

"I'll go exploring," said the mole. "I have many holes under these rocks."

While the mole slipped under the biggest rock his friends bent their heads down to hear his digging noises. They waited a long time.

"I wonder why he takes so long?" said the rabbit. "Perhaps he has found the treasure and is smelling it."

"Or he went to sleep," yawned the hippopotamus. "I am so tired of waiting I'll sit down for a while." He almost sat on the mole who was coming out of a hole behind him.

"Have you found anything?" asked the Happy Lion.

"Nothing. Nothing but bugs and worms."

"Then it's in the moat," said the hippopotamus. "I knew it all along. Let me go and take a look."

"Please don't," said the duck. "You would splash most of the water out. I will go. Watch me dive."

Every time the duck's head bobbed up above the water to breathe, the Happy Lion rushed to him to ask,

"Have you found anything?" But the duck was soon in again, leaving some bubbles on the water. At last he came out.

"Nothing," he said. "Nothing but weeds, frogs, and fish."

DENVER
PUBLIC LIBRARY
OCT 1971
CITY & COUNTY OF DENVER

"Before some know-it-all tells us that the treasure is in the hollows of the trees," said the squirrel, "let me tell you that there is nothing in there but peanuts. The peanuts children give the Happy Lion on Sundays. He can't eat peanuts, so I store them there for the winter."

"If you don't mind my saying so, my little fellow," said the hippopotamus, "you have been too busy storing your peanuts to pay attention to what's in the tree holes."

"Why don't you go in and look for yourself, my fat friend," answered the squirrel.

"Well said," said the mole. "That big thing accused me of going to sleep when I was straining myself digging under the rocks. Those who do nothing always criticize those who work."

"I agree with the hippo," said the bear. "Those little beasts are busybodies. The mouse to the contrary, I still think that the treasure is under the house. That's obvious as I said before . . . Ouch! How dare you!" the bear roared suddenly as the mouse jumped up and bit his nose.

"Well done, mouse," whistled a sparrow. "Get him! Get him!"

"All *I* can say," said the owl from the top hole in a tree, "I have never seen so many scatterbrains all talking at once and saying nothing."

"Don't you play the wise owl," snapped the magpie. "It's a fact that owls are wise only in fairytales."

"And it's a fact that magpies are thieves," screeched the owl. "They steal everything that shines. The treasure may well be in your and your sisters' nest."

At that moment, the Happy Lion climbed slowly up on his highest rock and looked at the assembled company with great sadness.

"My dear friends," he began . . . but the noise now was so loud that no one heard him.

"PLEASE," cried the raven with his loudest croaky voice. "In the name of my ancestors, who were lawyers as all you noisy and quarrelsome beasts well know, I ask for silence. Our Happy Lion wants to speak to you."

"I do not know what folly has come over you," said the Happy Lion. "You know I love you all; I know you love me and really love each other. This, I believe now, is the reason for our happiness here. And, I wondered as you were quarreling, perhaps this is also the secret treasure our friend François talked about."

"By all my ancestors," cried the raven, dancing joyously on top of a rock, "how stupid of me not to have guessed all this myself. Indeed your secret treasure, Happy Lion, is not in the moat, in the tree holes, under the house, or under the rocks. It is not in the magpies' nests. It is hidden in your own heart. To know how to love and to be loved, *that* is the treasure which makes you and those who know you so happy."

"Yes, truly, my Happy Lion," said François, who had been watching these doings from the lion's house, "you have guessed your secret treasure."

"And even if it shocks my ancestors, who were all lawyers, as I hardly need tell you now," added the raven, "I say what's hidden inside of you can be put into a will. I shall write our Happy Lion's will. It will say that from this time forth, he will bestow to everyone, for ever and ever, the secret of happiness."

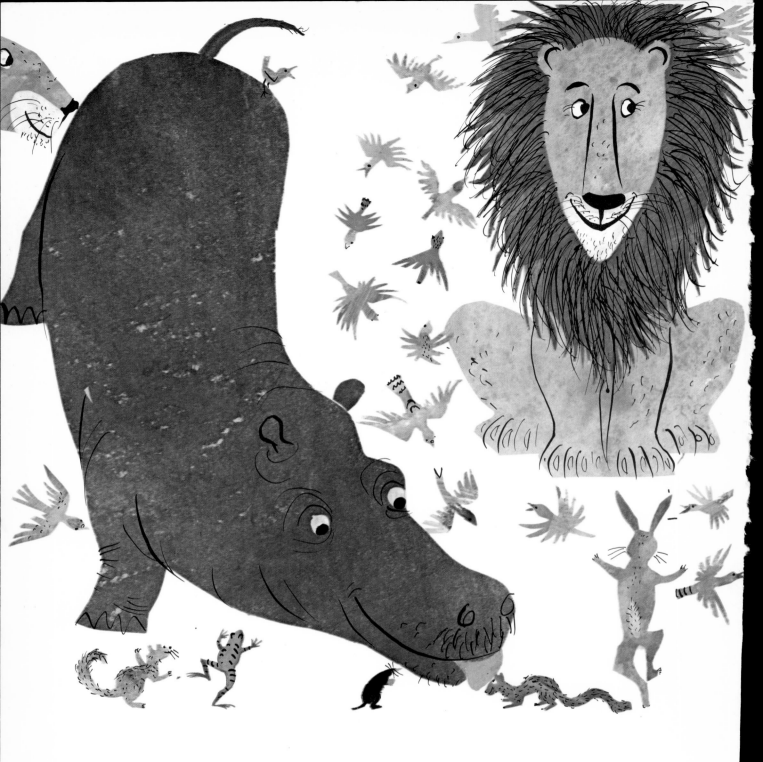

All the beasts now danced and sang together with joy. "How we love you, our dear Happy Lion, how we love you and love each other."

The bear kissed the mouse, the mole kissed the hippopotamus, the hippopotamus kissed the squirrel, and even the owl kissed the magpie.

"What a beautiful day that was," said the Happy Lion to the lioness that evening. "I am so especially pleased I found the secret of our happiness."